GOLDEN ARROW

The story of the
7th Indian Division.

The Naval & Military Press Ltd

Published by

The Naval & Military Press Ltd
Unit 5 Riverside, Brambleside
Bellbrook Industrial Estate
Uckfield, East Sussex
TN22 1QQ England

Tel: +44 (0)1825 749494

www.naval-military-press.com

*In reprinting in facsimile from the original, any imperfections are inevitably reproduced
and the quality may fall short of modern type and cartographic standards.*

THE VICTORIA CROSS

NAIK NAND SINGH, 1/11th Sikh Regiment

Naik Nand Singh led his men up a steep knife-edged ridge in the Kalapanzin Valley and, although wounded in the thigh, dashed forward and took the first trench single-handed at the point of the bayonet. He then crawled forward alone under heavy fire. A grenade wounded him, but he took the second trench, again at the bayonet point. A few minutes later, the whole of his section having been killed or wounded, Naik Nand Singh charged on to a third trench, captured it and killed the occupants with his bayonet.

NAIK GIAN SINGH, 4/15th Punjab Regiment.

Firing his tommy gun and hurling grenades, Naik Gian Singh made two lone charges against the Japs astride the Kamye-Myingyan road. When a Punjab platoon came under very heavy fire, Nk. Gian Singh ordered his machine gunners to cover him as he rushed enemy fox-holes. Our tanks moved up and came under fire, but Nk. Gian Singh, who had sustained several wounds, annihilated a Jap anti-tank gun's crew, capturing the weapon single-handed. He then led his section in clearing all enemy positions until the end of the action.

LIEUT KARAMJEET SINGH JUDGE, 4/15th Punjab Regt. Posthumous

Lt. Karamjeet Singh Judge displayed superb gallantry near Myingyan. Concealed enemy bunkers in the reverse slopes of broken and untankable ground, constantly shelled and machinegunned our troops, who were held up by five from bunkers not seen by our tanks. Lt. Karamjeet Singh Judge time and again went forward through heavy fire to recall our tanks to deal with bunkers indicated by him. Leading successive infantry charges, he wiped out ten Jap positions already battered by our tanks and was mortally wounded, but his men, inspired by his example went on to clear the whole area.

RIFLEMAN LACHHIMAN GURUNG, 4/8th Gurkha Rifles

Rifleman Lachhiman Gurung's platoon was surrounded for three days and two nights by the Japs at Taungdaw. The enemy hurled innumerable grenades at the position, two of which Rfn. Lachhiman Gurung picked up and hurled back. While holding a third grenade the fingers of his right hand were blown off. Disregarding his terrible injuries he loaded and fired his rifle with his left hand as the enemy formed up to rush the position. Wave after wave of fanatical attacks were thrown in by the Japs but all were repulsed with heavy casualties.

UNITS which served with the DIVISION during the period AUGUST 1943 until DECEMBER 1945.

INFANTRY

33rd Indian Infantry Brigade.
  1st Battalion Queens Royal Regt. 4/15th Punjab Regt. 4/1st Gurkha Rifles.

89th Indian Infantry Brigade.
  2nd Battalion, Kings Own Scottish Borderers. 1/11th Sikh Regt. 4/8th Gurkha Rifles. 1/9th Royal Jat Regt. 1st Burma Regt. (From August 1944 – April 1945.)

114th Indian Infantry Brigade.
  1st Battalion Somerset Light Infantry. 2nd Battalion South Lancashire Regt. 4/14th Punjab Regt. 4/5th Royal Gurkha Rifles. 2/6th Gurkha Rifles.

ADDITIONAL UNITS

Divisional Reconnaissance Battalion.
  7/2nd Punjab Regt.

Machine Gun Battalion.
  Machine Gun Battalion Frontier Force Rifles.

Divisional Defence Battalion.
  2nd Baroda Infantry (I.S.F.)

DIVISIONAL CAVALRY
  3rd Gwalior Lancers (I.S.F.)

ARTILLERY
136th & 139th Field Regiments. R.A. 14th Anti-tank Regt. R.A. 6th (M) Anti-tank Regt. I.A. 25th & 30th Indian Mountain Regiments.

ENGINEERS
62nd, 77th and 421st Indian Field Companies, I.E. 303rd and 331st Field Park Companies I.E.

SIGNALS
7th Indian Division Signals.

MEDICAL
44th, 54th and 66th Indian Field Ambulances. 32nd Field Hygiene Section.

INDIAN ELECTRICAL and MECHANICAL ENGINEERS
6th, 39th and 133rd Indian Infantry, Workshop Companies. 7th Indian Division Recovery Company.

ROYAL INDIAN ARMY SERVICE CORPS
60th & 61st Companies. (Divisional Transport) 20th, 57th, 63rd and 65th Animal Transport Companies. 29th, 30th, 31st and 32nd Indian Composite Platoons.

MISCELLANEOUS
A56th Field Security Section. 2nd & 14th Platoons Burma Intelligence Corps. 7th Indian Division Ordnance Sub Park. 7th Indian Division Mobile Veterinary Section. 7th Indian Division Provost Unit. 7th Indian Division Postal Unit.

BURM

LUMDING
KOHIMA
NAGA HILLS
UKHRUL
KANGLATONGBI
SILCHAR • IMPHAL
UPPER CHINDW
BISHENPUR
LOGTAK LAKE
INDIA
TAMU
MANIPUR
CHINDWIN
AIJAL
MAWLAIK
TONGZANG
CHOCOLATE SIALUM VUM
STAIRCASE TIDDIM
KENNEDY PEAK KALEWA
FORT WHITE No.3 STOCKADE
KALEMYO
MYITTHA
YE-U
RANGAMATI
CHIN HILLS
KALADAN
GANGAW
MONYWA
LOWER
CHINDWIN
TILIN
PAUK • PAKOKKU
MYIN
MAYU
PALETWA
MYITCHE • NYAUNGU
LETSE PAGAN
x NGAKYEDAUK PASS SINGU Mt POPA
• BUTHIDAUNG SEIKPYU KYAUKPADAUNG
MAUNGDAW
GWEGYO

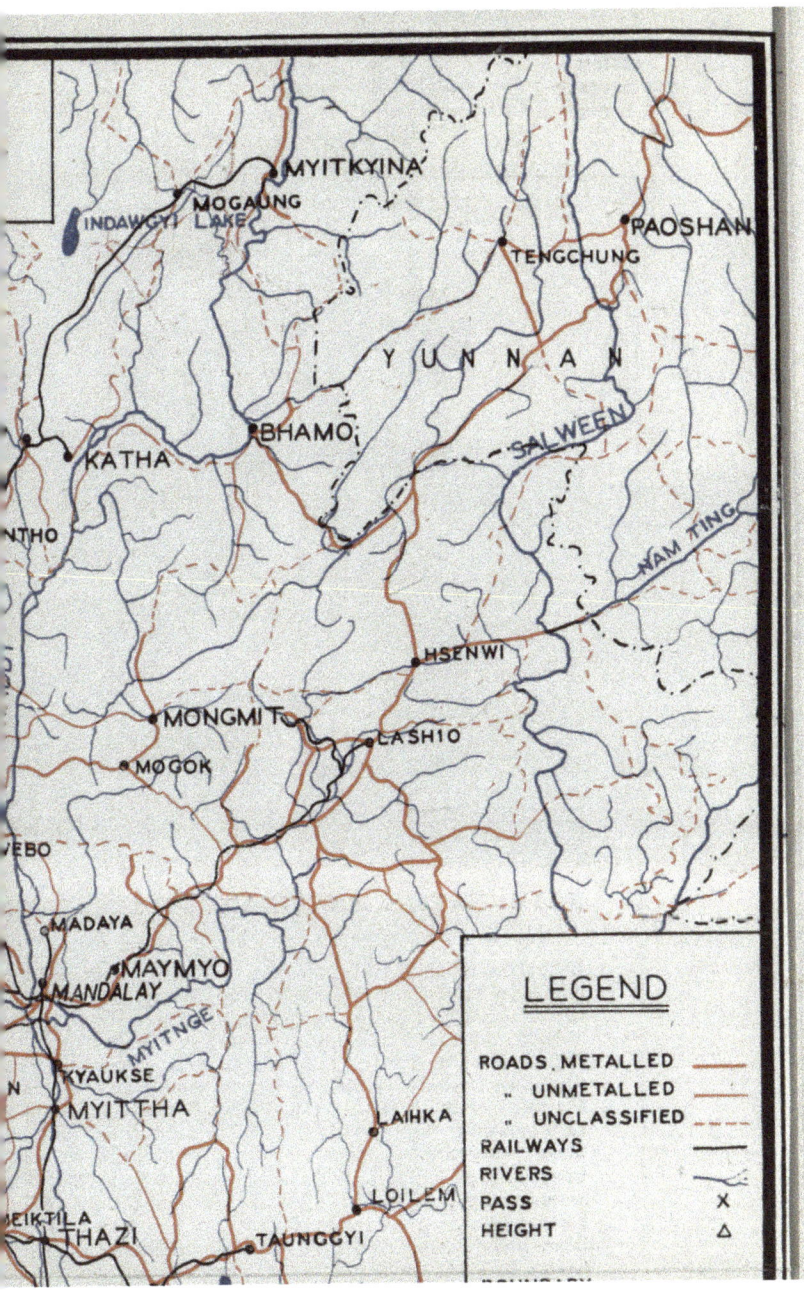

BUTHIDAUNG
MAUNGDAW
GWEGYO
RATHEDAUNG
YENANGYAUNG
MINBYA
MON
MINBU MAGWE
AKYAB
MYEBON
PADAN
TAUNGDAW
ARAKAN
AN
YOMAS
IRRAWADDY
KYAUKPYU
THAYET
RAMREE ISLAND
KAMA ZALON
TAUNGUP
PROM
CHEDUBA ISLAND
TAUNGUP PASS
SANDOWAY

BAY

OF
HENZADA

BENGAL
BASSEIN

BASSEIN

MOUTHS OF THE IRRAWADDY

DIVISIONAL COMMANDER — 1

Maj. Gen. (now Lt. Gen. Sir) F. W. MESSERVY, K.B.E., C.B., D.S.O., commanded from 30th July 1943 until 7th December 1944.

DIVISIONAL COMMANDER — 2

Maj. Gen. G. C. EVANS, C.B.E., D.S.O., commanded from 29th December 1944 until 6th February 1946.

BRIGADIERS
COMMANDER ROYAL ARTILLERY.—Brig. T. HELY, C.B.E. D.S.O.

33rd INDIAN INFANTRY BRIGADE.
Commander. Brig. G. COLLINGWOOD, D.S.O., Brig. VICKERS, D.S.O. and left in jeep, Lt. Col. (now Brig.) L.H.O. PUGH, D.S.O.

★

89th INDIAN INFANTRY BRIGADE.
Brig. (now Maj. Gen.) W. A. CROWTHER, C.B.E., D.S.O.

★

114th INDIAN INFANTRY BRIGADE.
Brig. H. W. DINWIDDIE.

★

A.D.M.S.—Col. W. A. BURKI., C.B.E.

SUPPLY DROPPING

GOLDEN ARROW

Introduction

TO the 7th Indian Division in the Arakan campaign of the Spring of 1944, when it held out against Jap encirclement for three weeks in its defensive boxes east of the Mayu ridge, went the honour of first showing the world that Allied forces in the South East Asia theatre had the whip hand of the Jap and that the so-called master of the jungle could be thrashed on his own ground.

Here, for the first time, too, as Dakotas roared over the green heights of the Mayu ridge to drop parachuted supplies to the beleaguered garrisons, was demonstrated the technique of air supply which set at nought the Japanese method of encirclement and severing lines of communication—a manoeuvre to which there had previously been no successful answer.

This classic operation displayed the future pattern of the Burma war, repeated first on a large scale in the defensive battle of the Imphal plain a month later when 4th Corps was supplied by the unhampered road through the skies, demonstrated again on an even larger and more daring scale in the second Wingate expedition with the 3rd Indian Division, and finally used throughout the successful offensive of the Fourteenth Army in the Spring and early summer of 1945 which broke the Japanese Armies in Burma.

But the brief burst of fame which came to the 7th Division in February 1944 does not represent the full accomplishments of this hard fighting formation.

Led first by General Frank Messervy, later to command 4th Corps in the drive on Meiktila and Rangoon, and later by Maj.-General G. C. Evans, who, as a brigadier in the 5th Indian Division, had commanded the " Admin Box " at Ngakyedauk, the Division has played a full part in the defence of India's borders and the final liberation of Burma.

It fought at Kohima, Imphal and Ukhrul. It was the springboard of the drive of 17th Indian Division from the bridgehead above Pagan on the Irrawaddy to Meiktila which was the decisive operation of the Burma war. It liberated the oilfield area of Chauk and Yenangyaung, completed the destruction of Japanese remnants in the river valley and retreating elements from the Arakan, and even during the monsoon months in Burma after the capture of Rangoon, was hammering the Jap on the banks of the Sittang river— still fighting and fighting hard.

The 7th Indian Division, though mobilised for war only in the spring of 1942, bears a time honoured title. For it was the 7th Indian Division that bore the standard of the Indian Army through Mesopotamia to Egypt in the last Great War. And even before its mobilisation when it formed part of North Western Army, it was playing its role in the greater war effort as a training formation which frequently had to surrender large numbers of its best men for service in other theatres of war.

The Division's mobilisation and transformation into a full-fledged fighting formation bore early testimony to the capacity of India Command to produce the material in manpower and equipment which would give us decisive superiority over the enemy.

Though during this mobilisation period of the spring and summer of 1942, the Division was stationed in a remote region of the Hazara district of the North West Frontier Province, the arsenals of Northern India fed the tools of war through the narrow supply line which crept up through the mountain from the nearest railhead.

By the winter of the same year, the Division was ready, if not for war, to take the field as a fully organised fighting formation. On the banks of the Indus river—the historic frontier of India in the North—the Division completed its preliminary training.

With its role changed now from a reserve Division which was to be available for service in any theatre of war, to a formation which was destined for the war against Japan, the Division went into jungle training in the Central Provinces of India.

Here during the spring and summer of 1943, it learnt the technique of jungle war and laid the foundation for its later mastery of the Japanese.

The beginning of the road to Victory. Entrance to the formidable Ngakyedauk Pass.

THE GOPPE PASS

Part I—The Arakan

IN the autumn and winter of the same year, the Division, now under command of General Messervy, moved east to challenge the enemy on the eastern frontier of India. For its fighting symbol it had adopted the Golden Arrow—an arrow with its war head tempered for battle and flighted and hafted to hit square the high mark of achievement.

With one brigade over the Goppe Pass on East Mayu before the turn of the year, the Division began the pressure advance down the Mayu peninsular which was to force the Japanese back on to the line of the Maungdaw-Buthidaung road.

Deployed with it in 15th Indian Corps battle order was the famous veteran 5th Indian Division, moved from the Middle East to Burma to demonstrate in the East the ability of the Indian soldier to meet and beat any enemy in any theatre of war.

Maungdaw, the river port in the estuary of the Nat river, fell to the 5th Division in January 1944, and with our forces pressing down on the Maungdaw-Buthidaung road from the foothills of the Mayu ridge, the 7th Division moved in full strength to east of the ridge to form a two Divisional front.

The Ngakyedauk pass—later so memorable, was constructed by the Division's sappers—one of the best miniature engineering achievements of the Burma war—and the Division's life-line from the main line of communication running south from Chittagong through Bawli was this corkscrew one way road through the virgin jungle of the Mayu ridge.

In the Kalapanzin valley the Division deployed with one brigade pressing down on the Maungdaw-Buthidaung road west of the river, and another on the east bank poised for a long left hook on Buthidaung.

Overlooking the road the 2nd Battalion The King's Own Scottish Borderers took possession of "Able" feature, later held by men of the 4/1st Gurkha Rifles in a vicious month-long battle when night mule convoys running the gauntlet across the open paddy were the only means of supply. The eastern foothills of the Mayu ridge were cleared south of the Ngakyedauk Pass.

But to the east the Japanese Command was preparing its march on India which was to break the Allied forces on the Indo-Burma border and open the road to the plains of Assam and Bengal.

In practice, this offensive fell into two distinct stages—first the Arakan offensive, second the drive on the Imphal plain. The intention of the enemy was to launch an offensive in the Arakan, draw 14th Army reinforcements to that area, and thus put in the main attack on Imphal. Had this Arakan offensive been successful, we would never have been able to release the 5th and later the 7th Divisions from the Arakan to assist in breaking the Japanese siege of Imphal.

His plan was to encircle and destroy the 7th Division east of the Mayu ridge, then cut the main line of communication from Chittagong to Bawli behind the 5th Division on west Mayu and drive it into the sea.

For this purpose he deployed a force of several thousand men with gunners, sappers and ancilliary units. In command of this force was Col. Tanabashi.

The plan was to attack the 7th Division from the rear and annihilate it. The next stage was to be a concentration of the main force on the Ngakyedauk Pass while another detachment got over the ridge and cut out our line of communication in the region of Bawli. The whole force was then to descend on the 5th Indian Division and complete the destruction of Allied forces in the Arakan.

This ambitious plan was by no means a surprise to the 14th Army Commander, General Slim, and his staff. The technique of resistance against encirclement by the formation of defensive boxes had been worked out and the preliminary arrangements made for the maintenance of these isolated forces by air supply. To the north of Chittagong, the 26th Indian Division was under the commander's hand.

On February 3rd leading elements of the task force came into contact with troops of the Seventh Indian Division east of the Kalapanzin river.

On 7th February confused fighting raged to the north of the eastern end of the Ngakyedauk pass where men of the 2nd Battalion The King's Own Scottish Borderers, the 4/8th Gurkha Rifles, and the 7/2nd Punjab, with tanks of the 25th Dragoons, temporarily held back the encirclement threat.

Divisional headquarters was overrun in the early hours of the morning of February 6th after Indian State Cavalry (Gwalior Lancers) had reported the presence of Japs in Taung Bazar away to the north and east. The brunt of the attack was borne by the Divisional signals. Staff officers and clerks joined in the confused fighting. General Messervy led out a party of his staff by wading down a chaung. Divisional headquarters, practically intact, fought its way out and retired to the famous " Admin Box " at the foot of the Ngakyedauk Pass.

Meanwhile other groups of the task force with elements of the I.N.A. had penetrated towards the main line of communication west of the Mayu ridge and were endeavouring to hamper the movement of supplies. The road was under fire in several places. Briasco bridge was attacked, but was quickly repaired. The Ngakyedauk Pass was closed by the Japanese task force.

In the " Admin Box " 7th Divisional headquarters with large numbers of Corps and service troops and elements of a brigade of the 5th Indian Division including three companies of the 2nd Battalion West Yorkshire Regiment, prepared a perimeter in the dry dusty bowl of paddy fields east of the foot of the pass, crammed with mules, men, tanks, vehicles and guns.

The order had gone out to stand firm. The Dakotas began to wing their way towards the gallant garrisons with supplies. The 7th Division prepared to defy the enemy to the last.

For 18 days enemy aircraft, infantry and long range guns tried to hammer the " Admin Box " into submission. From surrounding hills mortars and machine guns fired into the " Box ". Constant attacks night and day went in against the troops holding the perimeter.

At the southern and eastern face of the " Box " the Japs astride the Ngakyedauk pass were in positions pressing right down on to the perimeter.

The MDS here was raided and the wards became a battleground, with the Japs using the hospital as a battle headquarters for 36 hours before they were thrown out.

The hospital was then moved back towards the foot of the pass, where in bamboo rigged shelters in a chaung, it tended the sick and wounded of the whole of the " Box " garrison, at one time holding as many as 500 patients.

Under constant danger the doctors carried on. Even the dental surgeon, wounded in the face and arm, took his share of the work in the wards.

Meantime, forces were advancing to the relief of the

beleaguered 7th Division. From the north over the Goppe Pass, the leading elements of the 26th Indian Division moved down, while from the west the 5th Indian Division cracked open the Ngakyedauk Pass. From the "Box" Brigadier Evans sent out men of the 2nd Battalion West Yorkshire Regt. and the 2nd Battalion King's own Scottish Borderers with tanks of the 25th Dragoons to meet the relieving forces.

Tanks of the 25th Dragoons, working from the western side, roaring up and down the dizzy curves of the pass in clouds of white dust, supported infantry of the 4/7th Rajputs, the 2/1st Punjab and 1/18th Garhwalis (of 26th Div.) to break through the Japanese ring. Air strikes by Vengeance dive bombers reduced Hill 1070—a conical feature overlooking the centre of the pass and, encircled by a mixed force of Rajputs and Garhwalis, the Jap garrison was driven off. Again with air support, men of the 4/7th Rajputs captured "Sugar Loaf" Hill, on the North Eastern edge of the "Box".

At 10-30 in the morning of the 23rd February the adjutant of the 2/1st Punjab greeted a Scottish soldier from the 7th Division on the roadway of the pass. Mopping up of isolated elements of the enemy on both sides of the pass went on.

Two days later the first ambulance convoys rolled out escorted by armoured cars. Within a few hours the patients were evacuated to hospitals in Bengal by ambulance planes. The "Box" had been relieved. The weary garrisons greeted their deliverers with joy and told tales, tragic, gallant, humorous, of the great siege.

The Japanese had lost heavily, 500 bodies were picked up round the box alone. Split into scattered remnants the vaunted Tanabashi task force was methodically reduced. The fighting in its early stages had cost them dearly. Now they were without supplies, cut off and disintegrated—the plight into which they had hoped to plunge the 7th Division. The back of the enemy offensive in the Arakan had been broken.

It was the proud boast of the 7th Division that at no stage did their forward line substantially change during the enemy offensive. East of the Kalapanzin, 114 Brigade composed of the Somerset Light Infantry, 4/14th Punjab and 4/5th Royal Gurkha Rifles had stood its ground and withdrawn only its feelers. On the Maungdaw-Buthidaung road 33 Brigade held on to " Able " while the tide of battle whirled around them to the north.

The Golden Arrow Division, having faced its crucial test, once again prepared for the offensive. The line of the Maungadaw-Buthidaung road still had to be secured before the monsoon.

Early in March, under a thunderous night barrage, men of the 1/11th Sikhs and the 4/15th Punjab swept down towards the road. With them moved tanks of the 25th Dragoons and sapper detachments to build tank crossings over the chaungs that served the route.

By dawn on the following morning the vital objectives had been secured. The 1/11th Sikhs proving themselves for the first time in action as a whole battalion had seized "Poland" and held it against counter-attack. The 4/15th Punjab were on " West Finger " and the Queens were south of the road on "Cain," opposite the gallant Gurkhas, still fighting their battle on " Able."

A few days later the Sikhs swept through the forward Punjabi positions, cheered on by their fellow warriors in the Sikh company and drove the Japanese from " East Finger " —the last remaining feature before Buthidaung. Riding on the tanks of the 25th Dragoons they swept into Buthidaung and found that the enemy had fled from this shattered town.

It was here that the 11th Sikhs secured the first V.C. for the Golden Arrow Division. A force of enemy 40 strong infiltrated into a position overlooking the road to Buthidaung in the rear of our forward positions. The enemy had to be driven out at all costs. Naik Nand Singh commanded the leading section of the platoon which was to retake the position. The enemy was entrenched on the top of a knife-edged ridge. Coming under fire, he was wounded in the thigh but took the first trench at the point of the bayonet. Wounded again in the face and shoulder by a grenade, he stormed a second position singlehanded and killed its occupants. Then with most of his section killed or wounded he took on a third position, again with the bayonet, and wiped out the enemy.

To the North, on the west bank of the Kalapanzin, another stern action was fought by the 7/2nd Punjab. Here on " Bulge ", a similar situation developed. A party of Japanese, this time more than a hundred strong infiltrated on to the " Boomerang " feature where battalion headquarters was located. The Colonel led the first attack with battalion headquarters men on what was estimated to be a minor nuisance party and was killed by a grenade. Troops were recalled from the forward positions to deal with the enemy. Their attempts to retake the position failed. Finally the position was recaptured by a composite force from all companies of the battalion with the aid of tanks. More than a hundred Japanese were killed in their bunkers, and five medium machine-guns were captured. General Messervy visited the battalion after the battle and told the men that he had never witnessed such brave and desperate fighting.

With Buthidaung captured, the brigade east of the Kalapanzin moved down on Japanese positions still held north of the line of the Maungdaw-Buthidaung road. Tanks were ferried across the river on sapper constructed rafts and the 4/14th Punjab drove the enemy from their positions on

Long Ridge. Preparations were made to drive the enemy, too, from their long held strongpoint at Kyaukit which had defied dive bomber and artillery bombardment. But here, isolated by withdrawals, the Japanese pulled out and a section patrol of the 5th Royal Gurkhas on the eve of the attack entered it unopposed.

Before the 7th Division finally completed its task in the Arakan, the Japs made one more bid against them. A suicide party of 400 coming up West Valley penetrated for a second time to the " Admin box " and Divisional' headquarters staff once more found themselves manning slit trenches on the perimeter. The 2nd Punjab held the raiding party off a vital feature overlooking the box and the liquidation of the enemy force was completed by the 11th Sikhs, Garhwalis and Lincolns of the 26th Division which had by then taken over at Buthidaung.

THE JAP WHO LIVED — attended by M.O. — AND THE JAP WHO DIDN'T. Gurkhas walk past.

THE "ADMIN BOX"

THE NGAKYEDAUK PASS, constructed by the Division's sappers, showing one of the many bends.

BRITISH GUNNERS prepare to fire.

MULES toil up with supplies to forward positions.

THE "ADMIN" BOX. A view of the tank area, showing a Dakota dropping parachutes with much-needed supplies.

A PARACHUTE glides to earth. Another camera shot taken in the 'Box'.

AT THE FOOT OF "AMMUNITION HILL". Another view of the tank area within the perimeter of the "Admin Box".

AMBULANCE CONVOY prepares to leave the 'Box' with wounded after the battle had ended.

MORE VITAL SUPPLIES drop from the sky to sustain the garrison.

PAGAN

Part II—Kohima, Imphal, Pakokku, Pagan.

GRAVE news was coming from the north, where 4th Corps was now facing the full weight of the enemy "invade India" offensive. The Japanese plan having been foiled in the Arakan, the 5th Indian Division was free to reinforce the northern line and did its famous "fly out" to the Imphal plain.

Next came the turn of the 7th Division to take up the battle against encirclement again. 33 and 114 brigades went north to Dimapur, 89 brigade joining the 5th Division in the Imphal plain.

Round Kohima, the men of the Golden Arrow Division gave their lives to break the Jap stranglehold on our land line of communication from Imphal to Dimapur. The 1st Battalion Queens, the 4/15th Punjab and the 4/1st Gurkha Rifles fought in these battles. Memorials on these bloody heights testify to the sacrifices made by the men of the Seventh Division. "Jail Hill" was a Seventh Division battle and the Division, too, captured the final Kohima stronghold at Naga Village.

Kohima was cleared, but the fight down the road to link with the beleaguered garrison in Imphal still lay ahead.

While the 2nd British Division fought down the axis of the road, to the 7th Division went the task of carrying out an outflanking movement to the east along the Jessami track.

The monsoon broke as they pressed down towards Ukhrul across mountains 4000 feet high and through flooded mountain streams. Air supply was impossible and Jeeps ran "round the clock" shuttle services along perilous tracks to keep the advancing troops supplied.

Japanese forces which had made the drive on Kohima were now defeated and retreating. As the Division advanced stray parties of hungry, tattered and bewildered enemy fell into their hands.

In the Imphal plain 89 brigade of the 7th Division, which had joined forces, together with 139 Jungle Field Regiment, with the 5th Division, fought actions around Kanglatongbi. Once again the 1/11th Sikhs proved themselves with the 2nd Battalion, King's Own Scottish Borderers and the 4/8th Gurkha Rifles in the attack on Kanglatongbi ridge, where the Scots went into action with pipes playing and the Sikhs carried out a brilliant march to the rear of the enemy.

In the Imphal plain the battle neared its end. The Japanese attempts to break through from the south along the Tiddim and Tamu roads had been defeated.

The last stage was the liquidation of the force that had attempted to reach Imphal from the east from the direction of Ukhrul. Pressure from the north by the elements of the seventh Division and along the axis of the road by troops of Fourth Corps drove the enemy back towards the Chindwin.

The 7th Division brought its participation in the 1944 campaign to an end by driving straight from Ukhrul to Laung Chaung, cutting the Jap line of retreat and line of communications. Over jungle covered mountains rising to 6,500 feet they completed the rout of the enemy.

The battle of the Imphal plain ended, the 5th Indian Division and the 11th East African Division carried on the pursuit of the broken " invade India " armies of Japan down the Tiddim and the Tamu roads, to link up finally in November at Kalemyo.

West of the Chindwin the Japs had been driven down the Myittha valley to Gangaw by the mystery force of the Lushai brigade which emerged from the hills where it had operated on the right flank of the 5th Division's advance.

Resting at Kohima, the Golden Arrow Division, now under command of Maj.-General G. C. Evans, was called into battle towards the end of December. Its sappers had been the first to move and had constructed a new "Ngakeydauk" over a range of hills bordering the Chindwin at Thaungdut. The 19th Indian Division used this pass later as part of the "road to Mandalay."

But before Christmas came further orders for the sappers of the Golden Arrow Division. With part of 136 Field Regiment they moved 250 miles south to engineer a new road from the Manipur river, crossing at Sinaung Myauk, below Kalemyo, down into the Myittha valley.

THE UKHRUL ROAD. Body of dead Jap and debris strewn over abandoned vehicle.

While the sappers blasted and bulldozed their way through virgin jungle on a forty mile diversion which concealed our movements from the enemy remaining in the Myittha valley, the first guns of the 136 Field Regiment winched and hauled by "quads" reached Gangaw and were deployed against the Jap stronghold.

The sappers and gunners were the advance force of not only a Divisional but a Corps concentration which was the prelude to the decisive operation of the Burma war, the thrust into the heart of central Burma by the drive on Meiktila.

The Division was on the move, spread over three hundred miles of road from Kohima to Tamu and beyond. At this time the planning staff was fighting a battle with figures, for to provide road lift for an entire division including mule companies was no mean task.

The first stage of the march was to take them to Gangaw. From Gangaw they were to move south 150 miles to the banks of the Irrawaddy. The move was secret. All Divisional signs were blacked out. The use of wireless was forbidden. This concentration of 7th Division, to be followed by 17th Indian Division at a later stage, was the master stroke of the 14th Army.

The achievements of this trek to the banks of the Irrawaddy were phenomenal. All services played a distinguished part —for it was largely a service task. One mule company marched all the way from Kohima to Myitche more than 400 miles—and arrived with all its animals in good condition after a trek which would have done credit to an explorer. The Divisional RIASC found itself faced with the lifting of men and mules and supplying at one time units spread over 8,000 square miles of country. In this they had the assistance of air supply. Divisional signals laid over 800 miles of field cable in six weeks to maintain communication without wireless. The IEME leapfrogged its workshop companies down the march route to keep the Division on the move.

Operationally at this stage the Division's commitments were not great. Gangaw had fallen in the first week in January to men of the Chin Hills battalion of the Lushai Brigade after the biggest airstrike yet seen in the Burma war, which tore great rents in the enemy's jungle stronghold on the bank of the Myittha river.

28 East African Brigade took over the advance down the Gangaw valley. This was a picked screen, for the intention of the 14th Army Commander at this stage was to persuade the Japanese that the whole of 4th Corps had crossed the Chindwin and were headed for Mandalay. They were to assume that this East African brigade was part of the 11th East African Division which had chased them out of the Kabaw valley. Behind this deception screen the build-up of 4th Corps in the Myittha valley was to take place.

While the East African brigade moved south on the general axis of the road in the direction of Pauk, General Evans deployed his forces behind them with the object of obtaining a quick grip on the north and west banks of the Irrawaddy at the point where the river turns south after its confluence with the Chindwin.

33 Brigade was still moving down the tenuous and rapidly deteriorating line of communication from Kohima to Kan—north of Gangaw—a distance of 350 miles.

89 Brigade group on an all pack basis with Mountain Artillery in support was therefore sent off on a long left hook south of Gangaw between the Myittha and the Chindwin.

On the extreme left flank moved the Divisional reconnaissance battalion of the 7/2nd Punjab, with the Lushai Scouts.

Supplied entirely by air the 7/2nd Punjab moved through the rugged country on the east bank of the Myittha, marching 200 miles in four weeks to reach the Irrawaddy at Pakokku.

89 Brigade group, consisting of the 1/11th Sikhs, the 2nd Battalion Kings Own Scottish Borderers and the 4/8th Gurkha Rifles, moved south from Gangaw to cut the road from Tilin to Pauk, and to capture Pauk itself.

114 Brigade moved behind the East Africans. At Lessaw the 4/14th Punjab broke an attempt by the Japs to capture the Tilin air strip. The brigade then moved east towards Pakokku.

Here in the first week of February, stiff fighting for the possession of Pakokku took place, in which battalions of the 4/5th Royal Gurkha Rifles, and the 7/2nd and 4/14th Punjab were engaged against 214 Regt. of the famous 33rd Japanese Division. Pakokku was strongly defended and the fighting on the outskirts and in the town lasted a week before the enemy garrison was subdued with the loss of some 350 men.

Unknown to the Jap, who was completely mystified about our movements and appreciated that the whole of General Messervy's 4th Corps was across the Chindwin and headed for Mandalay, the 14th Army plan for the breaching and turning of the Irrawaddy line was nearing its climax.

The 19th Indian Division was breaking out of its bridgehead at Kyonkmyaming, in the face of heavy counter-attack; the thrust of the 20th Indian Division across the river at Myinmu was launched, to be joined later by the 2nd British Division crossing further east. The battle of the Irrawaddy line was on, General Slim struck.

While the southwards advance went on, 33 Brigade of the Division had been training at Gangaw for the crossing of the Irrawaddy.

Assault boats, rafts and sapper equipment had been moved south down the line of communication. Detailed air reconnaissance had been made to determine the best place for the crossing. Every hazard had been weighed and every detail of this vital operation worked out.

THE "ADMIN BOX". For eighteen days of unremitting enemy
out, while Dakotas at great peril conti

attack, and fighting of unparalleled savagery, the heroic garrison held
inued to drop supplies until relief arrived.

So far there was no indication that the enemy had any suspicion of our plan to cross the river and drive on Meiktila. But to make assurance doubly sure, the deception shadow play went on.

The East African brigade, having reached Pauk, pushed on to Seikpyu on the west bank of the river opposite the oil town of Chauk with the object of making it appear that we were aiming a direct thrust at the oilfields area. From the heavy counter-attacks which were thrown in this area it is apparent that the Jap swallowed the bait.

The place selected for the Seventh Division's crossing was opposite Nyaungu, just north of the ancient Burmese capital of Pagan. At this point the river was 2,500 yards wide and treacherous with shifting sandbanks.

On the far side were high cliffs broken by the fissures of dry nullahs. At the foot of these nullahs were our "D-day" landing beaches.

BUSHIDO! A Japanese gives up to men of the 2nd. Baroda Regt.

Every method was used to deceive the Japanese, that a crossing was to take place at Pakokku. Tanks were used here for the first time in these operations, and no movement South to Myitche was allowed by day. So successful was this feint that Japanese patrols reported the whole of the Division moving on Pakokku.

In the early hours of the morning of February 14th a company of the South Lancashire Regt.—specially selected for this task because of their training in combined operations —climbed into their assault craft and rowed silently across the river. It was pitch dark. A moonless night and a silent approach had been chosen to make the surprise complete.

At this moment, the plan which had been the result of weeks of detailed work and preparation, and on which the success of General Slim's whole strategy for the turning of the Irrawaddy line depended, almost hung by a thread.

The leading troops reached the far bank and were safely and secretly across. Dawn, however, was breaking and throwing a pearly light over the dark river as the second flight in outboard engined craft were some 200 yards from the further bank.

Jap machine gunners from caverns in the face of the cliffs opened up. Vicious spouts of water splattered up around the boats. Some were hit and men began to swim ashore. The enemy—too late—had awoken to his danger and was endeavouring to deny us our foothold on the far bank.

But the plan had been made to meet this contingency. Aircraft appeared and dived at the enemy positions. Columns of smoke mushroomed into the sky. Indian and British gunners opened up and bush fires blazed and smoked on the far bank. Tanks of the 116 Regt. R.A.C. (Gordon Highlanders) with their 75's and machine gunners of the Frontier Force Machine Gun Battalion with their Vickers, blazed away across the mile wide river.

Men of the 4/15th Punjab and the 4/1st Gurkhas crossed in succeeding waves followed by the 1st Burma Regiment.

By nightfall on the first day the whole of the assault brigade was across. The thread had not snapped.

Thereafter the bridgehead expanded rapidly and according to plan. In the following days men of the Burma Regt. winkled the Japs out of the old catacombs in Nyaungu where they had taken refuge, and by February 16th the bridgehead was 6000 yards broad and 4000 yards deep and the vehicles stores and equipment of two brigades were pouring across.

Further south, the 11th Sikhs, crossing the river in country boats after an initial setback, had captured Pagan, the ancient city of the five thousand pagodas. Sappers went to work lifting mines and repairing bridges.

NAGA VILLAGE. *Final Kohima stronghold of the Japanese, captured by men of the Division.*

IMPHAL, UKHRUL, PAKOKKU, PAGAN

A view of the vast expanse of the IMPHAL PLAIN, seen from the UKHRUL ROAD.

THE UKHRUL ROAD. A tank on patrol moves round the tortuous bends.

JESSAMI TRACK. Bulldozer clears way for traffic.

JESSAMI TRACK. Sappers construct roadway.

PAKOKKU. Troops advance into the outskirts of the village.

THE IRRAWADDY CROSSING. 4/1st Gurkha Rifles cross the river. The effects of shell-bursts can be seen on the far bank.

North of NYAUNGU. 4/15th Punjab go across the Irrawaddy on 14th February 1945. Smoke on the far bank is caused by air and artillery bombardment.

The other side of the Irrawaddy, showing the caves in the cliffs which were fanatically defended by the Japanese.

SUPPLIES and VEHICLES are transported across the river on rafts.

South-West of PAGAN, Sikh patrol charges Jap foxhole.

PAGAN AREA. Gurkha patrol advances cautiously.

OVERLOOKING THE IRRAWADDY, with smoke rising from the far side. Digging on outpost position.

PAGAN. A view of the ornate pagodas which were a feature of the town.

YENANGYAUNG OILFIELDS

Part III—Myingyan, Yenangyaung, Sittang.

THE bridgehead gained, the 17th Indian Division's mobile column swept through to Meiktila. The Golden Arrow Division had done the first part of its job—to launch this sudden and decisive blow at the enemy's vitals in Central Burma.

For the hard-fighting 7th Division, much gruelling work lay ahead. The bridgehead had to be held secure. South at Seikpyu on the western bank the Japs had reacted strongly to the East Africans advance. To the north on the eastern side of the river, the Japs were in considerable strength and occupied the important river port of Myingyan, a railhead too for the metre gauge railway running east to Meiktila and beyond.

The operations to clear the approaches to this town and to drive out the enemy garrison brought the Golden Arrow Division two more V.C.'s, both awarded to Sikhs from the same regiment—the 4/15th Punjab and making three Sikh V.C.'s in the Division.

On the Kamye-Myingyan road early in March, Naik Gian Singh, leading a section of his platoon in an attack on a village which would give us control of essential water points in the area, rushed the enemy fox holes, firing his tommy gun and hurling grenades. He killed four enemy in the main weapon pit. Wounded in this affray, he rushed forward and annihilated the crew of a Jap anti-tank gun which was engaging our tanks and captured the gun single handed. Then leading his section he cleared the remainder of the enemy positions. Twenty enemy bodies were found in this area, the majority of which fell to the Naik and his section. Though wounded and ordered to the RAP the Naik requested permission to stay until the successful completion of the action.

It was again the 15th Punjab which made the assault on Saka and opened the gates of Myingyan four and a half miles to the north. After an artillery pounding, the Jat company rushed the village and the enemy retreated to a wooded area to the north. With two troops of tanks the Jats went in pursuit and found the enemy a company strong, well established in a big dry pond where bunkers linked by a network of tunnels gave them a strong position.

Led by their Subedar, the Jats rushed the bunkers, winkling the Japs out of their tunnels and killing more than 40 of the enemy.

Myingyan fell after a four day battle in which the brilliant team work of infantry, sappers, artillery and tanks decided the issue.

North of the town the Sikh company of the 7/2nd Punjab had crossed the Irrawaddy and occupied the airfields. By night, attacks of the 4/15th Punjab crossed a heavily mined and shelled chaung, to enter the town by night. With the Japs continuously shelling an area of not more than 7000 square yards, sappers cleared mines in the chaung and the Jat company on the following morning enlarged the bridgehead on the far side.

In the cotton mill area, tanks bumped across the open ground while the infantry chased the Japs from bunker to bunker. Men of the 4/1st Gurkhas meanwhile had entered the railway station and occupied the marshalling yards. During the night they were supplied by our tanks.

The southern half of the city was cleared on the following, day when the 4/15th Punjab battled 600 yards up the heavily mined streets. The Japs were driven back into the jail area. On the last day of the battle the Jail was hit by an air strike bombarded by artillery and tanks and the Japs fled westwards to be shot up by tanks lying in wait for them as they fled.

It was on the outskirts of this city that Lt. Karamjeet Singh Judge won his posthumous V.C. He led charge after charge on enemy bunkers and wiped out ten Japanese positions which had been battered by tanks. Time and again he dashed forward to recall tanks to deal with hidden bunkers. Finally he was mortally wounded, but his men went on and cleared the area. The citation described him as an " outstanding leader of matchless courage."

While Myingyan was being cleared, the Golden Arrow Division was striking with mobile columns in the region of Mount Popa, to the south of the bridgehead area.

Armoured cars, artillery and mobile infantry, in small, hard-hitting formations, comprised these columns. Japanese defences in the Mount Popa area were probed and wherever the Jap tried to come forward, he was stopped.

West of the river in the Letse area, the East African brigade was bearing the brunt of strong Japanese counter-attacks. Here the 4/14th Punjab were continuously in action over a period of two months.

In one counter-attack, the Japanese, 500 strong, renewing their assault after one determined effort had been beaten back, penetrated 200 yards inside the perimeter.

While Indian field gunners cracked down just ahead of our troops machine gunners from the Frontier Force Machine Gun Battalion and Mahratta Anti-Tank Regt.—a Four Corps unit—drove the Japs out at the bayonet point, killing 250 of the enemy and wounding more than a hundred.

While the Golden Arrow Division was fighting these actions and hammering the enemy north of the oilfields area, the 14th Army plan on the Irrawaddy moved to completion. Mandalay had fallen, the link up with the 17th Indian Division in Meiktila had been made and the drive for Rangoon was on.

The 7th Division's next task was to be the capture of the oilfields area and the advance down the Irrawaddy valley towards Rangoon. Their collaborator in this drive was another hard fighting Division—the 20th which struck south from the Meiktila area to the bottom of the oilfields pocket through Magwe to Prome.

Meanwhile, 89 Brigade, which was disposed to prevent a Japanese advance on the bridgehead from the Chauk direction was beating back determined Japanese counter-attacks. At Milaungbya, four miles north of the Singu the 8th Gurkhas killed 250 Japs—the record bag being 94 in one day, while 2nd Battalion Kings Own Scottish Borderers killed over 100 in one battle alone.

With this holding operation in progress, General Evans swung his other brigade in a wide sweep to the east together with 268 Independent Brigade who had joined the Division.

First aiming mark for the Golden Arrow Division was Kyaukpadaung, 30 miles South of Pagan, the key rail and road focal point and for long, an important enemy communication base.

1st Battalion of the Queens Royal Regiment which had now rejoined the Division with the 4/15th Punjab and the 4/1st Gurkha Rifles moved by night on the town. Four miles distant, the British battalion flung a screen across the road, while Gurkhas out-flanked to the east and the 4/15th Punjab occupied a ridge south of the town, and blocked the escape route to Gwegyo.

The following day on the west the 4/15th Punjab were strongly counter-attacked amongst the scrub-covered country and a fierce battle raged all day. Tanks of the Carbiniers assisted the Gurkhas forward and they established themselves half a mile west of Kyaukpadaung. With the town virtually encircled, a heavy airstrike went on in the railway station area and the artillery joined in. A short battle followed in the station area where the Gurkhas drove the Japs from their last remaining positions. The enemy fled south, pursued by the shelling of our guns.

General Evans did not wait. He drove on to Gwegyo—19 miles from the oil centre of Chauk. In their retreat the Japs had made plentiful use of mines and booby traps and to the sappers fell the task of clearing these dangerous obstacles.

The 4/15th Punjab pushed on and holding a road block half way to the village, provided a base for another out-flanking movement to the south by the British battalion. Gurkhas, aided by sappers with beehive charges cleaned up in the cliffs in the railway station area where the Japs were still holding out in spite of shelling from our tanks.

The rapidity of the move gave the enemy no time to reorganise and nearly 200 Japs, the whole complement of the garrison, were killed.

Next to fall was Singu which was captured by 4/8th Gurkhas of 89 Brigade pressing down from the north.

Singu is intersected by a chaung, and the Gurkhas surrounded the northern half by moving at night round the west of the town unheard by the enemy garrison. Though on the following day, the Japs tried to rush the Gurkha positions in the pagoda area, where our troops were pinned down by violent sniping, the Gurkhas, with machine gunners of the Frontier Force Machine-Gun Battalion, beat off the attacks and the Japs fled through South Singu by the only available escape route.

While the battle for Singu raged the Japs began evacuating Chauk. Some got away across the river, while others tried to get down stream in boats, where they were shot up by our river patrols.

As our troops, fresh from the victories of Gwegyo and Kyaukpadaung, entered Chauk, the Burmese population came out of their houses and lined the streets to greet their liberators. Most of the oil wells and machinery were intact. And so fast was the advance that the Japanese had been forced to dump their stores in the river and had even burnt 200 bags of rice to prevent them falling into the hands of the needy Burmese. Several guns and machine guns fell into the hands of the brigade.

Forty eight miles south of Chauk lay Yenangyaung—the chief town of the oilfields area. The brigade moved rapidly south and the Queens were soon three miles outside the town.

Tanks of the Carbiniers moved up to help the advance, while the 4/1st Gurkhas, advancing across country, got astride a ridge overlooking the town from the river side. Hunting the enemy out of their cave hideouts, the Gurkhas next flushed 200 Japs bolting for the river and seeking cover in the cliffs on the river bank. Artillery fire was brought down on them and by nightfall few were alive.

Tanks and the 4/15th Punjab on the east of the town were meeting stiff resistance, but the Queens had now forced their way into the centre and Jap opposition had dwindled to sniper activity. A final Gurkha charge on the following morning cleared the last remaining Jap stronghold. Five 75mm guns, six anti-aircraft guns, 3,000 rounds of artillery ammunition formed the booty.

The last oilfield town cleared, the attention of General Evans was turned to the west bank of the Irrawaddy where a considerable force of Japs had accumulated and were joined by retreating elements from the Arakan.

Heading 114 brigade which had moved south from Letse down the west bank, was the 4/5th Royal Gurkha Rifles which soon gained contact with the enemy, who were driven south into the area of the Shandat Forest.

Meanwhile General Evans had switched 89 Brigade which had moved down the east bank across the river at Kyauke, to join in the extermination battle on the western bank and a series of operations followed in which 114 Brigade was the hammer driving the Japanese southwards on to the anvil prepared by 89 Brigade.

At Taungdaw two companies of the 4/8th Gurkha Rifles of 89 Brigade were surrounded by more than 500 Japs in thick jungle country and for five days there was heavy fighting in sweltering heat and intermittent monsoon downpours. The 1/11th Sikhs came to their aid and on the last day the Japs were in full retreat.

Over 300 dead Japanese were counted on the Gurkha perimeter. It was in this battle that Rifleman Lachhiman Gurung, 4/8th Gurkha Rifles, won the Victoria Cross.

Later the 1/11th Sikhs, after a strenuous jungle march, during which they wiped out a complete party of 73 Japs in one swift battle, pushed south to Kama.

A big annihilation battle was now imminent. Rangoon was occupied, the 14th Army was firmly in control of the Rangoon-Mandalay road, and the situation in the Irrawaddy valley on the Rangoon-Prome road was rapidly being cleared up.

In the Pegu Yomas between the two road axes was a considerable force of Japs which had been left behind in the rapid advance of the 5th and 17th Indian Divisions towards Rangoon.

The only course open for those Japs on the west bank o the Irrawaddy was to try and break out to the east and join their comrades in the Pegu Yomas. To stay on the west bank was to be harried, trapped and eventually destroyed.

The 1/11th Sikhs, with the 2nd Battalion Kings Own

Scottish Borderers and 268 Independent Brigade, established themselves at Kama on the west bank, continuing to drive the enemy south, while at Zalon on the east bank eight miles north of Prome the Japs attempted to establish a bridgehead and hold open an escape route to the east. Here the 4/1st Gurkhas, the 4/15th Punjab and the Queens put a ring round the bridgehead and squeezed in. Against the northern tip, the Punjabs put in fierce attacks. The Gurkhas were attacked in a succession of waves, but threw a desperate enemy back with heavy casualties. Further to the east were the 2/8th Punjab and the 1/19th Hyderabad of 20th Division who were attached to 7th Division for this operation.

To prevent enemy ex-filtration the 2nd Battalion Kings Own Scottish Borderers were moved from Kama to line the Prome road. A party of fifty officers and men of the Kings Own Scottish Borderers massacred 130 of the enemy with rifle and machine gun fire as they tried to escape from the bridgehead across the Prome road.

The total losses of the enemy in the battle of the Zalon bridgehead was 1,500 killed and 70 prisoners. It was only a depleted and shaken remnant of the escaping forces that found its way into the Pegu Yomas to join up with their equally battered comrades.

By the end of June, the Golden Arrow Division, after a long and hard fought campaign, could claim 4,000 counted enemy dead, more than a 100 prisoners, and amongst its booty numbered three tankettes, 48 guns and several medium machine guns.

But the task of the Division was not yet finished. The Irrawaddy valley cleared of the enemy, the Golden Arrow Division moved east to the Sittang line in the misery of the Burma monsoon, during which fighting had to be done in waist-deep water and continued to batter the enemy into final annihilation and defeat.

Finally the Division was flown into Siam. It provided the first troops in South East Asia to enter enemy-occupied territory. It disarmed and concentrated 113,000 Japanese, many of whom had fought against the Division. It evacuated some 20,000 U.K. and Australian ex-prisoners-of-War, and succoured no less than 25,000 coolies who had been brought up from Malaya to labour on the Moulmein railway.

Thus concludes the story of a fighting formation, whose exploits and achievements will be an inspiration to posterity.

THE END

A Japanese General surrenders his sword in company with 23 others at BANGKOK on 11th January 1946.

YENANGYAUNG TO BANGKOK

YENANGYAUNG, the principal town in the oilfields area, lying 48 miles south of Chauk.

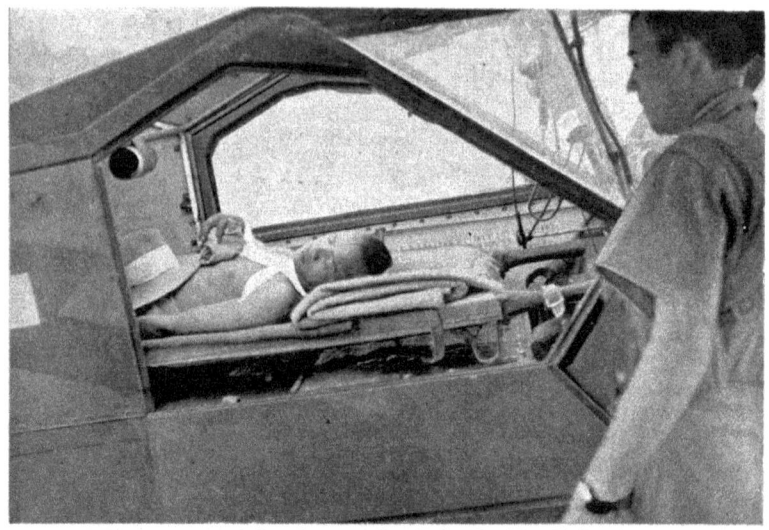

MINBU. A wounded rifleman of 4/8th Gurkha Rifles is evacuated in an L. V., piloted by a member of the 55th American Air Liaison Squadron.

BATTLE of the SITTANG BEND. A patrol of the Queens Royal Regt. during the battle near WAW.

BANGKOK. Men of the 62nd Indian Field Company built this Bailey bridge over the Menam river.

Guard of honour found by 1st Battalion Queens Regt. at the ceremonial parade for H. M. the King of Siam. Detachments of 4/14th Punjab and 4/5th Royal Gurkha Rifles also took part.

AT BANGKOK on 19th January 1946 H.M. the King of Siam takes the salute during the march past.

INDIAN DIVISIONS WON A FINE REPUTATION IN WORLD WAR TWO

Field Marshal Auchinleck, Commander-in-Chief of the British Indian Army from 1942, asserted that the British "*couldn't have come through both wars (World War I and II) if they hadn't had the British Indian Army*". British Prime Minister Winston Churchill also paid tribute to "*the unsurpassed bravery of Indian soldiers and officers*".

Between 1945 and 1947, the Director of Public Relations, War Department, Government of India, published a series of short publications covering the individual histories of the WWII Indian Divisions. They followed a consistent format, having between 44 and 48 pages within illustrated soft card covers. They have an average of 50 monochrome photographic illustrations, and each has a full colour centrespread depicting a scene from the Division's wartime operations (drawn by official war artists). They were printed at various presses in Bombay and New Delhi, and each contains at least one map.

As condensed histories they are useful – particularly those which relate to Divisions for which no other record was ever produced.

The British Indian Army during World War II began the war, in 1939, numbering just under 200,000 men. By the end of the war, it had become the largest volunteer army in history, rising to over 2.5 million men in August 1945. Serving in divisions of infantry, armour and a fledgling airborne force, they fought on three continents: in Africa, Europe and Asia.

This Army fought in Ethiopia against the Italian Army, in Egypt, Libya, Tunisia and Algeria against both the Italian and German Army and, after the Italian surrender, against the German Army in Italy. However, the bulk of the British Indian Army was committed to fighting the Japanese Army, first during the British defeats in Malaya and the retreat from Burma to the Indian border; later, after resting and refitting for the victorious advance back into Burma, as part of the largest British Empire army ever formed. These campaigns cost the lives of over 87,000 Indian service- men, while another 34,354 were wounded, and 67,340 became prisoners of war. Their valour was recognised with the award of some 4,000 decorations, and 18 members of the British Indian Army were awarded the Victoria Cross or the George Cross.

RED EAGLES
The Story of the 4th Indian Division
9781474537520

During the Second World War, the 4th Indian Division was in the vanguard of nine campaigns in the Mediterranean theatre, Egypt, Eritrea, Syria, Tunisia, Italy and Greece. The 4th Division captured 150,000 prisoners and suffered 25,000 casualties, more than the strength of a whole division. It won over 1,000 honours and awards, which included four Victoria Crosses and three George Crosses. Field Marshal Lord Wavell wrote: "The fame of this Division will surely go down as one of the greatest fighting formations in military history."

THE FIGHTING FIFTH
History of the 5th Indian Division
9781474537513

As described in much greater detail in Anthony Brett James's book 'The Ball of Fire', the division saw active service in East Africa, North Africa and Burma.

GOLDEN ARROW
The Story of the 7th Indian Division
9781474537506

The role of this division is also duplicated by a much larger work: the book by Brig. M. R. Roberts. However, this booklet gives a good account of Kohima and Imphal and the crossing of the Irrawaddy. In 1945, the division was flown into Siam, so becoming the first Allied formation to re-enter South East Asia.

ONE MORE RIVER
The Story of the 8th Indian Division
Biferno, Trigno, Sangro, Moro, Rapido, Arno, Senio, Santerno, Po, Adige

9781474537490

The 8th Indian Division started its overseas service in the Middle East in the garrisoning of Iraq and then the invasion of Persia to secure the oil fields of the area for the Allies, before moving to Italy in 1943. Landing at Taranto, it pushed up the length of the peninsula in a series of major battles: breaking the Sangro Line, forcing the Rapido and turning the defences at Cassino, breaking the stubborn German resistance at Monte Grande and, finally, forcing the Po River. It won four VCs, 26 DSOs and 149 MCs along the way. During the war the 8th Indian Division sustained casualties totalling 2,012 dead, 8,189 wounded and 749 missing.

BLACK CAT DIVISION
17th Indian Division

9781474537483

This formation was committed to Burma from the early days when the British were in full flight from the invading Japanese. It remained in Burma right through to the end, when the starving remnants of the Japanese Army were making their own desperate retreat.

TIGER HEAD
The Story of the 26th Indian Division
Arakan, Ragoon

9781474537452

This is a history of the division said later by the Japanese to have been the opponent which they most feared. The 26th held the Allied monsoon line in the Arakan during two such seasons, repulsing every attack launched against it. Later it made a series of leap-frog landings down the coast to clinch the issue in the Arakan. It was the first division to enter Ragoon, invading the city from the sea.

A HAPPY FAMILY
The Story of the Twentieth Indian Division, April 1942-August 1945

9781474537476

One of the few Indian divisions in the 14th Army trained specifically for the war in Burma. Raised in Bangalore in 1942, it commenced active operations in late 1943 and served from Imphal through to the end. It established the 14th Army's first brigade-head across the Chindwin and its second such brigade-head across the Irrawaddy. Its final task was to round up the Japanese in French Indochina.

THE TWENTY THIRD INDIAN DIVISION
"The Fighting Cock Division"
Burma, Malaya, Java

9781474537469

The Fighting Cock Division is well recorded in the book by Doulton. This book gives coverage of the heavy fighting at the Kohima Battle, the capture of Tamu, the reoccupation of Malaya in August 1945, and then its strange role on the island of Java – concurrently disarming the Japanese garrison, fighting the insurgent Indonesian nationalists, and caring for 65,000 former internees pending the arrival of a new Dutch administration.

TEHERAN TO TRIESTE
The Story Of The Tenth Indian Division

9781783317028

This History deals with the 10th Indian Div's exploits in Iraq (under Maj Gen "Bill" Slim) its role in the Libyan battles leading up to El Alamein, the following two years of garrison duties in Cyprus and Syria, and finally, its fighting services in the Italian campaign (from Ortona onwards).

THE STORY OF THE 25th INDIAN DIVSION
The Arakan Campaign
9781783317585

Formed in Southern India in August 1942 for defence of that area in case of Japanese invasion, the "Ace of Spades" Division had its baptism of fire in Arakan in February 1944. It served throughout the remainder of that campaign the climax being the battle of Tamandu.

Its victorious fight for the Kangaw roadblock was considered by many to have been the fiercest battle of the entire Burma war, while its liberation of Akyab was the first convincing proof to the rest of the world that the tide had turned against the Japanese.

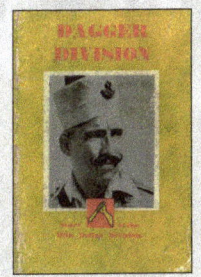

DAGGER DIVISION
The Story Of The 19th Indian Division
9781783317035

Raised in the late 1941, the 19th was the first "standard" Indian Division. Its troops were the first to breach the Japanese defence line in Burma and to raise the flag at Fort Dufferin. It crossed the Chindwin in November 1944, driving on to Mandalay and Ragoon during seven months of continuous fighting. The 19th's exploits are graphically described also in John Masters' personal memoir, *The Road Past Mandalay*.

www.ingramcontent.com/pod-product-compliance
Lightning Source LLC
Chambersburg PA
CBHW041928090426
42743CB00021B/3474